Apostolic Diet Plan for Women

A Faith-Based Biblical Guide to Clean Eating, Wellness & Spiritual Growth

Esther R. Hamilton

CW01563540

Gratitude

First and foremost, I give all glory, honor, and praise to the Almighty God, the Creator of heaven and earth, who is the giver of wisdom and the source of all life. Without His guidance, inspiration, and grace, this work would never have been possible.

I am deeply grateful to the Holy Spirit for leading me through this journey, teaching me how to combine biblical wisdom with practical healthy living. Every chapter, every verse, and every meal idea came together because of His gentle direction and constant reminders.

To my family—thank you for your patience, prayers, and encouragement. You stood by me through the late nights, endless note-taking, and countless edits. Your love gave me the strength to keep going.

To my friends, mentors, and spiritual leaders who inspired me to dig deeper into the Word of God—thank you for sowing seeds of faith, health, and discipline in my life.

Lastly, to every woman who will read this book: I wrote it with you in mind. You are precious to God, and it is my prayer that these teachings will renew your spirit, restore your body, and transform your daily walk with Him.

May the Lord bless you richly, keep you strong, and guide your steps always.

What Readers Are Saying

"This book opened my eyes to how biblical eating can truly transform health. I've never felt so spiritually and physically aligned." – **Mary L.**

"I followed the principles in this plan for just two weeks and noticed more energy, less bloating, and a deep sense of peace." – **Angela K.**

"It's not just a diet—it's a way to honor God with my body. The meals are delicious, simple, and deeply nourishing." – **Rachel P.**

"Finally, a diet plan that makes sense both spiritually and physically. I feel lighter, healthier, and closer to God." – **Deborah O.**

"The Apostolic Diet Plan helped me find balance between faith and healthy living. My body feels renewed, and my spirit is uplifted." – **Elizabeth A.**

Table of Content

CHAPTER 8: THE POWER OF FASTING
Types of Biblical Fasts
Fasting for Physical and Spiritual Breakthroughs
How to Start and Maintain a Fasting Lifestyle

PART 3: APOSTOLIC RECIPES & MEAL PLANS

CHAPTER 9: 7-DAY APOSTOLIC MEAL PLAN
Clean, Simple, and Nourishing Meals
Breakfast, Lunch, Dinner & Snack Ideas
Scripture for Each Day

CHAPTER 10: FAITH-BASED RECIPES FOR WOMEN
Breakfasts: Faith-Filled Mornings
Lunches: Light & Holy Midday Meals
Dinners: Comforting & Blessed Evening Meals
Snacks: Little Bites with Big Blessings
Dinners: Nourishing Evening Meals to End the Day with Peace
Herbal Teas & Healing Drinks

CHAPTER 11: RECIPES FOR FASTING DAYS
Light Soups, Broths & Juice Ideas
Fasting-Friendly Foods
Prayer & Fasting Journal Prompts

PART 4: SPIRITUAL GROWTH & ENCOURAGEMENT

CHAPTER 12: SPIRITUAL GROWTH THROUGH DIET
Eating with Gratitude
Renewing Your Mind Daily
Growing in Faith through Discipline

CHAPTER 13: ENCOURAGEMENT FOR THE APOSTOLIC WOMAN
Scriptures for Strength
Overcoming Discouragement & Temptation
Staying the Course with God

CHAPTER 14: CONCLUSION

INTRODUCTION

My Journey to the Apostolic Diet

I never imagined I would write a book like this. But the truth is—this isn't just a book. It's a reflection of my heart, my journey, and the deep desire to help women like you walk in wellness, strength, and holiness.

There was a time when I was constantly tired. I prayed, I served, I gave my all—but my body was failing me. I didn't feel healthy, and I knew something was missing. I asked the Lord to show me what I was doing wrong. And the answer was clear: "You're not taking care of the body I gave you."

That moment was a turning point.

I started searching the Bible—not just for spiritual guidance, but for health and healing. I began to see how God had already given us everything we need to nourish our bodies and spirits. From the clean food laws in Leviticus to the story of Daniel and his wise food choices, to Jesus Himself gathering around simple meals—Scripture opened my eyes to a whole new way of eating.

And more importantly, a whole new way of living.
That's how the Apostolic Diet Plan was born. It's not just about food—it's about obedience. It's about choosing wholeness over convenience, discipline over indulgence, and faith over fads.

This book is for the Apostolic woman who wants to align her body, mind, and spirit with God's plan. It's for the wife, the mother, the sister, the single woman, and the prayer warrior who wants to feel better, live longer, and grow closer to the Lord—through the way she eats and lives daily.

Inside these pages, you'll find more than recipes. You'll find encouragement, biblical truth, practical steps, and spiritual nourishment. Whether you're just starting or looking for a way to reset your health journey, this guide is here to walk with you—every step of the way.

I'm not a perfect woman. I still have days where I struggle. But I now know that with the Holy Spirit's help, and the wisdom of God's Word, I can choose better—and so can you.

Let's do this together.
With love and faith,
Esther R. Hamilton
Author & Sister in Christ

Why This Book Was Written for You

This book was written with you in mind—yes, you, the woman reading this right now.

Maybe you've been feeling tired lately. Maybe your body feels heavy, your mind is always busy, and you just don't feel like yourself anymore. Or maybe you're trying to eat better, live right, and stay strong in your walk with God, but you don't know where to start.

I know how it feels to serve God with all your heart, but still feel weak in your body. I know what it's like to pray, fast, and love God deeply—but still struggle with food, energy, and health. You're not alone. Many women in the Apostolic faith go through the same thing. That's why I wrote this book—to help us go back to the basics and care for our bodies the way God wants us to.

This book is not about rules. It's not about being perfect or following a hard diet. It's about learning how to eat simple, clean foods that honor your body and honor God. It's about choosing foods that help you feel strong, focused, and full of life—so you can keep doing what God has called you to do.

I also wrote this book for the woman who wants to grow spiritually. What you eat can affect how you feel, how you pray, and even how you think. When you eat better, you feel better. And when you feel better, you pray better, live better, and love better.

So if you've been searching for a way to care for yourself—body and spirit—this book is a small gift for you. It's full of truth, encouragement, and simple steps to help you start or continue your journey. Take your time with it. Don't rush. Just take one day at a time.

I believe God is calling His daughters to rise in strength—and it starts with how we live every day.

You are loved. You are seen. And you are not alone on this journey.
Let's walk together.

What You'll Gain from This Guide

This guide is more than just a book. It's a helper, a friend, and a gentle hand to lead you into a better way of living—one that feeds both your body and your spirit.

When you go through this book, you will learn how to take better care of your body with food that is clean, simple, and easy to prepare. You don't need to be rich or fancy to do this. You don't need special products or big kitchen tools. You just need a willing heart, a few basic ingredients, and a little bit of faith.

You will gain peace of mind. Many women today are confused about what to eat—there are so many diets out there, so many rules, and so many voices. This book brings you back to the Word of God and shows you a simple path you can follow with joy. No pressure. No guilt.

You will also gain strength. Not just in your body, but also in your spirit. When your body feels lighter, cleaner, and stronger, you will notice it in other parts of your life. You will sleep better. Think clearer. Pray with more focus. You will wake up with more energy and go through the day feeling less weighed down.

Most importantly, you will grow in your walk with God. Every part of this guide is written with love, prayer, and scripture. You will learn how food, fasting, and daily habits can help you stay connected to God—not just on Sundays, but every day.

You might be a busy mom, a single woman, a worker, or a homemaker. No matter where you are in life, there is something here for you.

So don't worry if you don't get everything perfect. This journey is not about perfection. It's about progress. Little by little. Step by step. Day by day.

By the time you finish this book, my prayer is that you'll feel more alive, more confident, and more in tune with who God has called you to be.

PART 1: FOUNDATIONS OF THE APOSTOLIC DIET

CHAPTER 1: WHAT IS THE APOSTOLIC DIET?

Origins and Meaning

Let's start with a simple question: What exactly is the Apostolic Diet?

The Apostolic Diet is not something new. It's not a trend or a modern food plan. It's a way of eating that goes back to the Bible and the early church—back to the time of the Apostles and the teachings they followed. That's where the word "Apostolic" comes from. It means "following the ways of the Apostles."

In those early days, people didn't eat processed food. They didn't have sugary snacks, fried fast food, or chemicals in their meals. They ate what God provided—natural, whole foods from the earth. Things like fresh vegetables, fruits, grains, herbs, fish, and clean meats. Their meals were simple, clean, and nourishing.

The Apostolic way of life is about holiness and discipline. It's about being set apart—not just in the way we dress or speak, but also in the way we eat and take care of our bodies. That's what this diet is all about. It's not just food—it's a lifestyle that honors God.

The Bible says in 1 Corinthians 10:31, "Whether you eat or drink, or whatever you do, do it all to the glory of God." That verse is the heart of this diet. We're not eating just to fill our stomachs. We're eating to stay strong, stay healthy, and stay useful for God's work.

The Apostolic Diet also respects God's instructions about clean and unclean foods, as seen in Leviticus 11. While we are not under the law like in the Old Testament, many Apostolic believers still follow these food guidelines out of respect and discipline. It's a personal choice, a way to stay focused and pure in every part of life—including food.

So, when we say "Apostolic Diet," we are talking about going back to simple, natural, Bible-based eating. We are choosing foods that give life, not harm. We are turning away from things that weigh us down and turning toward things that lift us up—spiritually and physically.

This is not about being perfect. It's about being intentional. It's about walking in wisdom and honoring God, one meal at a time.

How It Differs from Mainstream Diets

Let's be honest—there are so many diets out there today. Keto, vegan, low-carb, paleo, plant-based, detox this, cleanse that. It's easy to get confused. But the Apostolic Diet is not like these modern or trendy diets. It's different. Let me explain how.

First, the Apostolic Diet is based on faith, not fashion. It's not something made to make money or go viral. It's a way of eating that connects with our walk with God. It's built on Bible principles, not what's popular on social media. This diet is about honoring God with your food, not just losing weight or looking a certain way.

Second, there are no harsh rules or tricks. Many diets today are too strict. They tell you to count every calorie, avoid entire food groups, or follow hard meal plans that feel like punishment. The Apostolic Diet is simpler. It encourages natural, clean eating. You focus on what God made—whole foods, not fake foods. There's no need for expensive shakes, pills, or special bars.

Third, it doesn't only care about the body—it cares about the soul too. Most diets only talk about your weight, your shape, and how you look. But the Apostolic Diet cares about how you feel inside, how you pray, and how you grow in the Lord. This diet believes your physical health and your spiritual life work together.

Fourth, it teaches discipline, not just results. Many people want quick fixes, but the Apostolic Diet is more about long-term change. It helps you learn self-control, patience, and consistency—the same fruits of the Spirit we try to grow in other areas of our lives.

And lastly, it's personal and prayerful. With this diet, you can pray about your choices. You can fast with purpose. You can eat with joy and gratitude, not stress or guilt. It gives space for the Holy Spirit to guide you, even in your food.

So, while the world is chasing one diet after another, the Apostolic Diet calls you to slow down, go back to God's Word, and care for your body in a way that brings peace—not pressure.

This isn't just about food. It's about freedom. And it's for you.

Holiness in Eating

When we hear the word "holiness," we often think about how we dress, how we speak, how we worship, and how we live our daily lives. But have you ever stopped to think that holiness also includes how we eat?

Yes, what we eat and how we eat matters to God too.

As Apostolic women, we are called to live a life that is different from the world—a life that reflects God in every area. That includes our food choices. Holiness is about being set apart, not just in appearance, but also in how we care for the body God gave us.

Now, this doesn't mean you have to eat like a saint or be perfect at every meal. It simply means you become more mindful and intentional with your eating. You ask yourself:

- Is this food good for my body?
- Will this give me energy to serve God and take care of my family?
- Am I eating with self-control or just giving in to cravings?

That's holiness in eating. It's eating with purpose.

It's also about gratitude. When we stop to thank God before a meal, we're not just saying words—we're honoring Him.

We're remembering that food is a gift. We're showing respect to the One who provides. Eating without thought or care can lead to gluttony, waste, and even sickness. But eating with a thankful heart—that's holy.

Holiness in eating also means avoiding anything that pollutes the body. We stay away from processed junk, chemicals, and things that slowly harm our health. We choose clean foods, simple meals, and nourishing recipes that support the life God has called us to live.

When we eat with holiness, we are not following the world. We are following God. We are telling our flesh "no" when it wants too much, and telling our spirit "yes" when it seeks discipline and order.

This doesn't mean you can never enjoy your favorite foods again. It just means you enjoy them with balance, wisdom, and care.

So let's walk this path together—not with guilt, but with grace. Because every bite we take in faith, every meal we eat in wisdom, is another step closer to the life God wants for us.

CHAPTER 2: BIBLICAL PRINCIPLES OF EATING

Clean vs Unclean Foods (Leviticus 11)

One of the first places in the Bible where God talks about food is in the book of Leviticus, chapter 11. Here, God gives the people clear instructions about what foods are clean and what foods are unclean. These rules were not just for health—they were also about obedience, discipline, and being set apart.

Now, you might ask, "Are these food laws still for us today?"

The truth is, we are no longer under the Old Testament law. Jesus came and fulfilled the law (Matthew 5:17). But that doesn't mean we throw away everything God said. Many of these food rules were made to help the body stay strong and free from sickness. And many Apostolic women today still choose to follow them—not as a law, but as a wise and holy way of living.

Let's break it down simply.

✓ Examples of Clean Foods (Safe to Eat):

- Fish with fins and scales (like tilapia, mackerel, sardines)

- Chicken, turkey, and certain other birds
- Beef, goat, and lamb
- Fruits, vegetables, grains, and seeds

✗ Examples of Unclean Foods (Best to Avoid):
- Pork (like bacon, sausage, ham)
- Shellfish (like shrimp, crab, lobster)
- Catfish (no scales), shark, or other sea animals without fins and scales
- Animals that eat garbage or dead things (like vultures or pigs)

God gave these guidelines for a reason. Many unclean animals feed on waste or have toxins in their bodies. When we eat them, those toxins enter our bodies too. That's why some women who switch to clean foods feel lighter, healthier, and more energetic.

Again, this isn't about being legalistic or living in fear. It's about using wisdom. If God said something was unclean, there's usually a good reason behind it. Science has even proven that some of these "unclean" animals carry more disease and fat than others.

As Apostolic women, we want to treat our bodies with care. We want to eat what helps us—not what harms us. Clean eating is one way we show respect for the temple of the Holy Spirit— our body.

So when you choose clean foods, you're not just eating healthy. You're walking in wisdom and honoring God with your plate.

Fasting and Spiritual Discipline

Fasting is one of the most powerful tools we have—not just for the body, but for the spirit. As Apostolic women, we don't fast to lose weight. We fast to grow closer to God, to quiet our flesh, and to strengthen our spirit.

In simple words, fasting means letting go of food for a time so you can focus on God.

In the Bible, we see many people who fasted—Jesus, Moses, Esther, Daniel, and others. They fasted before making big decisions, during times of danger, or when they needed help and direction from God. And God always showed up.

Fasting is a spiritual discipline. That means it's something we do to train our spirit. Just like the body needs exercise to grow strong, the spirit also needs discipline to stay strong. Fasting helps with that. It teaches us to say "no" to our flesh and "yes" to God.

There are many ways to fast. Some people fast from morning till evening and eat one simple meal after sunset. Some avoid certain foods (like sweets or meat) for a number of days. Others do a full fast with only water or herbal teas. The key is to pray before you start and let God lead you in the way that's right for you.

Here's what fasting does:
• It clears your mind
• It strengthens your prayer life
• It helps break bad habits
• It brings healing to the body
• It opens your heart to hear from God

Fasting also works well with clean eating. When your body isn't full of junk or heavy meals, it's easier to fast without feeling weak or tired. Your body and spirit begin to flow together. You feel lighter, more alert, and more connected to the Holy Spirit.

But remember this: fasting is not about showing off. It's not to prove you're spiritual. Jesus said we should fast in secret (Matthew 6:16-18), with a humble heart, not to impress others.

So whether you fast once a week, once a month, or during special seasons, do it with prayer. Do it with love. And always end your fast with thanksgiving.

Fasting is not a burden—it's a blessing. A gift from God to help us walk in power and victory.

Jesus' Example of Eating and Fellowship

If there's one person we should look to when it comes to how to live, it's Jesus. And yes, that includes how we eat and who we eat with.

When you read through the Gospels, you'll notice something: Jesus spent a lot of time eating with people. He didn't rush meals. He didn't eat alone all the time. He used food as a way to teach, connect, and show love.

One of the first miracles Jesus performed was at a wedding feast in Cana, where He turned water into wine (John 2:1–11). He also fed thousands of people with just a few loaves of bread and a couple of fish (Matthew 14:13–21). And before He went to the cross, He sat down with His disciples to share the Last Supper—a simple but powerful meal that we still remember today (Luke 22:14–20).

These meals were more than just food. They were about fellowship, sharing, and purpose.
Jesus didn't overeat or fill His body with waste. He likely ate clean, natural foods—the kind of food available in His time: bread, fish, fruits, olive oil, honey, and vegetables. His eating habits were simple, balanced, and wholesome. He was never led by cravings, but by the Spirit.

One thing we can learn from Jesus is that eating is a spiritual act, not just a physical one. When we sit down to eat, we can take time to slow down, give thanks, and enjoy the moment.

We can invite others to the table, pray together, talk, laugh, and build stronger relationships. That's what Jesus did.

Another thing is that Jesus always gave thanks before eating. Whether it was a big meal or just a few loaves and fish, He paused to bless it. That simple act teaches us to be grateful, even when the food is little. Gratitude turns any meal into a holy moment.

So as Apostolic women, let's follow Jesus' example. Let's eat with intention, share our meals with others, give thanks always, and never let food become an idol.

Food is a gift. But fellowship—real connection—is what makes it even more meaningful.

CHAPTER 3: THE ROLE OF THE BODY IN APOSTOLIC FAITH

Your Body as God's Temple

Let's talk about your body—not from the world's view, but from God's view.

Many people think their body is just flesh and bones. But as an Apostolic woman, you need to understand that your body is so much more than that. Your body is God's temple.

In 1 Corinthians 6:19–20, the Bible says:
"Do you not know that your bodies are the temples of the Holy Spirit, who is in you, whom you have received from God? You are not your own; you were bought at a price. Therefore honor God with your bodies."

That verse is powerful. It means your body is not just yours to treat anyhow. God paid a price for you—through Jesus—and now, He lives in you. That makes your body holy and special.

Think about how people treat a church building. They sweep it. Clean it. Keep it neat and presentable. Now imagine that same care, but for your own body. Why? Because the Holy Spirit lives in you.

This is why eating well, resting properly, staying active, and even staying away from harmful things—like junk food, alcohol, or anything that defiles the body—is not just about health. It's about worship.

Every time you choose to eat clean, move your body, and avoid what will hurt it, you're saying:
"Lord, I honor You with this temple."

That doesn't mean you need to be perfect. Nobody is. But it means you try—daily—to take care of what God gave you. And when you fall short, you ask for grace and try again.

So from now on, don't think of healthy eating or taking care of your body as a burden. Think of it as part of your faith, part of your worship, and part of your walk with God.

Your body is a gift. Your body is a temple. And how you care for it is one way you show love and respect to your Heavenly Father.

Modesty, Purity, and Food

When we think of modesty and purity, we often think about clothing or behavior. And yes, those are important. But what many people don't realize is that modesty and purity also include what we eat and how we treat our bodies.

As Apostolic women, we are taught to dress modestly—not to show off or draw attention to ourselves. The same attitude should flow into how we eat. Modesty is about being humble, gentle, and disciplined—not only in appearance, but in lifestyle.

Let's be real—sometimes, the way we eat can become careless. We eat too much. We eat too fast. Or we eat without thinking about what's going into our bodies. But the same Spirit that teaches us to dress with self-respect also teaches us to eat with self-control.

Purity is not just about staying away from sin—it's about keeping your whole life clean, including your health. Eating clean, natural foods is one way to keep your body pure. Avoiding things that harm your health, like processed snacks, too much sugar, or fried food, shows that you respect what God gave you.

You don't need to eat like royalty or cook fancy meals to be pure or modest. You just need to keep it simple, clean, and balanced. That's the Apostolic way—a lifestyle that's not loud or wasteful, but thoughtful and disciplined.

Even how we serve and share food matters. Do we eat quietly and gratefully, or do we grab more than we need? Are we content with what we have, or do we always want more? Modesty in food is about being satisfied, not greedy. It's about feeding the body without feeding pride or fleshly desires.

This is not about shame. God is not punishing you for what's on your plate. But He is calling us to be aware—to live with purpose in every area. That includes what we eat, how much we eat, and the heart behind it.

So as you grow in modesty and purity, remember this: your plate matters too. Eat in a way that reflects who you are—a woman of faith, discipline, and grace.

Spiritual and Physical Self-Control

Let's talk about something that many of us struggle with—but don't always like to admit. Self-control.

It's not easy, but it's one of the most important things we need—both in our spiritual walk and in our daily life, especially when it comes to food.

Self-control means saying "no" when your body wants more than it needs. It means choosing what is right, even when it's not what you feel like doing. The Bible says in Galatians 5:22–23 that self-control is a fruit of the Spirit. That means the Holy Spirit helps us grow it, just like He helps us grow love, peace, and kindness.

Now, let's be honest. Sometimes the hardest battle is in the kitchen or at the dinner table. You're not alone. Many women, including faithful Apostolic women, deal with this too. You feel full but still want that second plate. You know it's not good for you, but the craving keeps calling. It's a real struggle.

But here's the good news: you don't have to fight this alone. The same Spirit that helps you pray, worship, and live holy can help you control your appetite. He can give you the strength to stop, to pause, and to choose better.

Spiritual self-control and physical self-control work together. When you learn to control your body, your spirit grows stronger. And when your spirit is strong, it becomes easier to say no to things that are not good for you.

Self-control is not just about food. It also includes your thoughts, emotions, habits, and lifestyle. But food is a good place to start. Why? Because we eat every day. It's part of our routine. And it's in those small daily choices that big changes happen.

So when you choose a healthier option, when you stop eating once you're full, or when you skip that sugary snack—don't see it as a small thing. See it as a victory. A sign that the Spirit is working in you.

Step by step, you'll grow stronger. Day by day, your body will learn. And through it all, your walk with God will become deeper.

Self-control is not about being perfect. It's about being obedient, disciplined, and free.

CHAPTER 4: BREAKING UNHEALTHY FOOD HABITS

Gluttony and Overindulgence

Let's talk about something that's often ignored but very real—gluttony.

Gluttony simply means eating too much, too often, or without self-control. It's not about enjoying food—God gave us food to enjoy. The problem is when food starts to control us, instead of us controlling it.

Sometimes, we don't even notice it. We just keep eating because the food is sweet, or because we're bored, sad, or stressed. Other times, we're already full, but we go back for more, just because it's there. That's not hunger. That's overindulgence.

Now, this is not about judging anyone. We've all done it. But as Apostolic women, we are called to live a life of discipline. That includes how we eat.

In Proverbs 25:28, the Bible says,

"A person without self-control is like a city with broken-down walls."

This means when we don't control ourselves—especially with food—we leave our bodies and our lives open to problems.

Gluttony can lead to:
- Tiredness
- Sickness
- Weight gain
- Weakness in prayer
- And even guilt or shame

But the good news is this: we can break free. With God's help, we can take back control.

Here are some small steps that help:
- Pause before eating. Ask yourself, "Am I truly hungry, or just emotional?"
- Eat slowly. Give your body time to feel full.
- Use smaller plates. It helps with portion control.
- Pray before meals. It sets your heart and mind in the right place.
- Practice saying no. Even to yourself. That's where strength grows.

Breaking free from gluttony doesn't happen in one day. But each small step is a victory. The goal is not to punish yourself. The goal is to live healthy, strong, and free—so you can do the work God has called you to do.

So the next time your flesh says, "Eat more," and your spirit says, "That's enough," listen to your spirit. That's where your strength is.

Sugar, Processed Foods & Addictions

Let's be honest—sugar is sweet, but it can trap you. So can processed foods like packaged snacks, soft drinks, white bread, and fried fast food. These things may taste good, but they often do more harm than good.

Many women today are struggling, not because they don't love God, but because their bodies are tired and weak from what they're feeding it every day. And the truth is, some of these foods are addictive. The more you eat them, the more your body craves them.

Sugar, for example, gives you a quick "high," but then crashes your energy. It can lead to weight gain, fatigue, mood swings, and even health problems like diabetes or high blood pressure. Yet many people can't go one day without it—not because they're greedy, but because their bodies have become used to it.

Processed foods are even worse. They are full of chemicals, fake flavors, too much salt, and hidden sugars. They fill your stomach, but starve your body. You feel full—but not truly nourished.

This is where discipline and awareness come in.

You don't have to throw everything out at once. Start small:

- Replace soft drinks with water or herbal tea
- Choose natural fruits instead of candy or cake
- Read food labels—if you don't know the ingredients, skip it
- Cook more at home using simple, fresh ingredients

You might feel weak in the first few days. Your body will fight back, asking for sugar or junk. That's normal—it's a sign that you're breaking the addiction. Don't give up. Drink more water, pray, and take it one day at a time.

Remember, food is not supposed to control you. You are the one in charge. You have the Spirit of God in you, and that Spirit gives you power to say no.

Healing starts when we say: "I want to feel better. I want to eat better. I want to live longer."

The goal is not perfection—it's progress. Each time you say no to sugar or processed food, you're saying yes to health, strength, and freedom.

And that's a beautiful thing.

Detoxing the Apostolic Way

When we hear the word "detox," many people think of expensive drinks, pills, or fasting challenges that promise fast results. But the Apostolic way of detoxing is different. It's not about trends or starving the body. It's about cleansing both the body and the spirit—gently, prayerfully, and naturally.

Our bodies are smart. God designed them to remove waste and toxins through the liver, kidneys, skin, and bowels. But when we overload our bodies with junk food, sugar, chemicals, and processed meals, these organs can get tired. That's when we start to feel heavy, bloated, tired, and even spiritually dull.

The good news? God also gave us natural foods to help our bodies reset.

Here are simple, safe ways to detox the Apostolic way:

• Drink more water. Water is life. It helps flush out waste, cleanses the system, and gives you more energy. Add fresh lemon or cucumber if you like.

• Eat more fruits and vegetables. They are full of fiber and natural healing. Apples, oranges, leafy greens, cucumbers, and carrots help clean the body gently.

• Cut back on sugar and processed foods. These clog the system. When you take a break from them, your body can rest and repair.

•   Include herbal teas. Ginger, mint, or lemon balm teas can calm the stomach and help the body release toxins.

•   Pray and fast. Fasting helps reset both body and soul. It's not about going hungry. It's about making room for healing—inside and out.

You don't need to buy anything fancy. Just return to the basics—natural food, clean water, rest, and prayer. That's the Apostolic way.

And remember, detoxing isn't just physical. As you clean your body, ask God to also cleanse your heart and mind. Let go of stress, bitterness, and fear. Use this time to read scripture, pray more deeply, and renew your focus.

Start small. Maybe do a 3-day gentle detox with fruits, vegetables, and water. Or remove sugar for one week and see how your body responds. The goal is not to punish your body—but to bless it.

Detox the way God leads you. Listen to your body. Trust the process. And do it all with a spirit of peace, not pressure.

PART 2: THE APOSTOLIC WOMAN'S WELLNESS PLAN

CHAPTER 5: CLEAN EATING GOD'S WAY

Whole Foods from the Bible

When we talk about clean eating in the Apostolic way, we are simply talking about eating foods that are natural, close to how God created them. These are what we often call "whole foods." Whole foods are not processed. They are fresh, simple, and full of life-giving nutrients. And guess what? The Bible talks about many of them.

Let's look at what people ate in Bible times. They didn't have canned food, chips, soda, or sugary snacks. Their meals were made with foods like grains, fruits, vegetables, fish, and clean meats. They also used natural oils like olive oil and drank water or fresh milk. These are the kinds of foods that kept them strong for long journeys and hard work.

For example, in the book of Genesis, we see that God gave Adam and Eve fruits and herbs for food. That was the original diet—fresh and plant-based. Later on, we read that people ate fish, lamb, goat, and sometimes beef. But God gave clear rules in Leviticus about what animals were clean and unclean. Clean animals were the ones allowed for food. This wasn't just about rules—it was about protecting our health.

Whole foods are still the best for us today. Fresh fruits like apples, dates, grapes, and figs were very common in the Bible. People also ate lentils, beans, and grains like barley and wheat. These are rich in fiber and help the body feel full and satisfied.

One thing we must remember is that our body is the temple of God. That means we should be careful about what we put inside it. Eating whole, natural foods is a way of honoring that temple. It's not about being perfect—it's about being intentional. Choosing God-made food over man-made junk.

So, when you go to the market, look for food that is fresh. Choose things with fewer ingredients. Cook meals with love, and eat them slowly. That's the Apostolic way—clean, simple, and led by God.

The Power of Water, Herbs, and Natural Healing

Let's talk about something very simple, but very powerful—water, herbs, and natural healing. These are some of the best gifts God has given to us. And the good thing? They are often free or easy to find. In the Bible, God didn't just give us food to fill our bellies. He gave us healing tools through nature. And when we understand how to use them, they can help us stay healthy—body, soul, and spirit.

Let's start with water. Water is life. It cleans the body inside and out. Our bodies are made up of mostly water, and without it, we can't survive. In the Bible, water was used for cleansing, for healing, and even for spiritual purification. Drinking clean water daily helps your body flush out toxins, helps digestion, keeps your skin fresh, and even helps your brain work better. If you want to feel better, one of the simplest steps is to drink more water.

Now let's talk about herbs. God made herbs for healing. Genesis 1:29 tells us that God gave us every herb bearing seed for our use. Herbs like ginger, garlic, bitter leaf, turmeric, cinnamon, and moringa are powerful. They are not just for cooking—they are also medicine. In fact, many of our grandmothers and mothers used herbs long before hospitals became popular. Herbal teas, for example, can help with digestion, sleep, stress, and boosting the immune system.

Natural healing is not about magic. It's about going back to the simple things God gave us—clean water, fresh air, good food, rest, sunshine, and natural herbs. These things work together to support the body and help it heal itself. When we avoid processed foods and start choosing natural things, we allow our bodies to become strong and balanced again.

So, don't overlook the power of nature. God created everything we need for our health and healing. It's right there—in a cup of clean water, in a pot of herbal tea, or even in a small garden at your backyard. Let us embrace these gifts and care for our bodies with what God has already provided. Healing doesn't always have to come from a hospital. Sometimes, it starts in your kitchen, with the wisdom God has already placed in your hands.

Shopping List of Faith-Based Ingredients

When we talk about clean eating in a faith-based way, we are simply going back to what God gave us from the beginning — natural, simple, and healing foods. Our bodies are regarded as the temples of the Holy Spirit, & what we put into them matters. That's why building a shopping list that reflects God's way of feeding His people is important. You don't need to overthink it. Just stick to what's natural, close to the earth, and as unprocessed as possible.

Here's a simple list of ingredients that line up with clean eating God's way:

1. Fruits and Vegetables (Fresh, Local, and Seasonal if Possible):
Think apples, grapes, figs, dates, pomegranates, olives, cucumbers, onions, garlic, and leafy greens. These are all mentioned in the Bible or are known to grow in biblical lands. They are rich in nutrients and are good for cleansing the body.

2. Whole Grains:

Barley and wheat were common in Bible times. Today, you can add oats, brown rice, and millet. Choose whole versions, not the white or refined ones. They give energy and keep you full longer.

3. Legumes:

Lentils and beans are powerful plant proteins. Lentil stew was even mentioned in the story of Esau and Jacob. These are great for clean, simple meals.

4. Nuts and Seeds:

Almonds, walnuts, flaxseeds, and chia seeds are small but mighty. They provide healthy fats and support brain and heart health.

5. Herbs and Spices:

Think of garlic, mint, dill, cinnamon, and cumin. Not only do they add flavor, but they also have healing properties. God created them for both food and medicine.

6. Healthy Oils:

Extra virgin olive oil is one of the best. It's mentioned many times in the Bible and is good for your heart and digestion.

7. Clean Proteins:

If you eat meat, go for clean meats like chicken, fish (with fins and scales), and eggs. Avoid animals that the Bible calls "unclean."

8. Water and Herbal Teas:

Clean water is life. Add in healing herbal teas like mint, ginger, or hibiscus to help cleanse your system gently.

When you shop, read labels. Avoid anything that's filled with chemicals, sugar, or things you can't pronounce. Keep it simple. God gave us all we need in nature. The closer your food is to how God made it, the better it is for your body and soul.

CHAPTER 6: DAILY MEAL GUIDELINES

How to Structure a Day of Apostolic Eating

Eating the Apostolic way is not just about what we eat, but also how and when we eat. A well-structured day of eating helps us stay balanced—spiritually and physically. This kind of eating is not stressful or complicated. It's simple, peaceful, and full of purpose. You don't need fancy foods or expensive items. Just real, clean food and a heart that wants to please God.

Let's break it down step by step:

1. Start your day with prayer and water.

Before you eat anything, begin with a short prayer. Thank God for a new day and ask Him to bless what enters your body. Then drink a glass of clean water. Water is a gift from God—it wakes up your body and helps flush out anything your body doesn't need.

2. Breakfast – Light and nourishing.

Keep your first meal of the day simple and gentle on your stomach. You can try fruits like apples, papaya, or bananas. If you prefer something warm, try a bowl of oats cooked with water and topped with honey or dates. Add a cup of herbal tea if you like.

3. Midday meal – Your main meal.

This is the time to give your body more strength. Think of vegetables, beans, lentils, fish, or whole grains. You can mix a little olive oil, herbs, and spices to make your meal tasty. Eat slowly and thank God for the food. Don't overeat. Just eat enough to feel satisfied.

4. Evening meal – Light again.

Dinner should not be heavy. The goal is to rest well at night, not struggle to digest food. Soups, steamed veggies, or small portions of clean protein like fish or boiled eggs are great choices. Add a glass of warm water or tea to help you relax.

5. Avoid late-night eating.

Try to stop eating at least 2 hours before sleep. Use that time for prayer, reading scripture, or quiet reflection.

6. End the day with thanksgiving.

Just like you began the day, end it with a thankful heart. Thank God for every bite you had, no matter how little or much.

Apostolic eating is simple. It's about honoring God with our bodies, choosing foods that give life, and being content. One day at a time, we grow stronger in faith and health.

Balanced Meals: Morning, Noon & Night

Eating in a balanced way means giving your body what it needs, at the right time of the day. Morning, noon, and night — each meal should serve a purpose. God didn't design our bodies to run on empty or junk. He created real food, and He gave us wisdom to eat in ways that keep us strong and full of life.

Morning – Start Light, Start Right

Your first meal for the day sets the tone for the day. You don't need to eat a heavy breakfast, just something simple and clean. Start with water — always. A glass of warm water with lemon helps wake your body gently and supports your digestion. After that, try something like fruit (apples, berries, or bananas), a handful of nuts, or a boiled egg. If you enjoy herbal teas, that's a good addition too. The goal is to nourish, not overload.

Noon – Your Main Meal

Lunchtime is the best time to eat your largest meal. At this time, your body is most active and ready to digest properly. Think of colorful vegetables, a good source of clean protein (like fish, beans, or lean meat), and some healthy fat (olive oil, avocado, or coconut oil). You can also add a little whole grain like brown rice or sweet potatoes. Keep it natural, fresh, and simple — just as God intended food to be.

Night – Light and Peaceful

Dinner should be the lightest meal of the day. Your body is slowing down and preparing to rest. So avoid anything heavy, oily, or processed. Go for a bowl of vegetable soup, steamed greens with a boiled egg, or a smoothie made from fresh fruits and water. A cup of warm herbal tea before bed is also great. Eat early enough so your food can digest before sleep.

The balance is not just about the types of food — it's also about listening to your body, eating slowly, and stopping when you feel satisfied. God's way of eating isn't about stress or rules. It's about peace, gratitude, and care.

Every meal is a chance to honor your body, honor your health, and honor the One who gave you both.

Portion Control with Biblical Wisdom

Eating is a blessing from God, but like all blessings, it should be enjoyed with wisdom. The Bible often talks about self-control, and this includes how much we eat. Proverbs 25:16 says, "If you find honey, eat just enough—too much of it, and you will vomit." This simple verse reminds us that even good food can harm us if we take more than our body needs.

Portion control is not about starving yourself; it is about eating enough to feel satisfied, not stuffed. In Biblical times, people ate to gain strength for their work, not just for pleasure. They enjoyed bread, fruits, fish, grains, and meat in reasonable amounts. Today, we have so much food available that it is easy to overeat without thinking. That's why we must be intentional.

A good way to start is to listen to your body. God designed our bodies to send signals when we are hungry and when we have had enough. Eat slowly, chew well, and pause to notice how you feel. If you feel comfortable and no longer hungry, stop eating—even if there is food left. This is one way to practice discipline, as mentioned in 1 Corinthians 9:27, where Paul talks about training his body and keeping it under control.

You can also use smaller plates or bowls. This naturally limits how much food you take and helps your eyes and stomach agree on what is "enough." Focus on filling your plate with more vegetables and lean proteins, and take smaller amounts of starchy or heavy foods.

Finally, remember that eating less is not only good for health but also an act of gratitude. When we avoid waste and eat wisely, we show respect for the food God has provided and for the needs of others. Just as Jesus taught about gathering only what was needed in the feeding of the five thousand, we too can learn to take only what we require for the moment.

Portion control is not a diet rule—it's a lifestyle choice rooted in self-control, gratitude, and respect for God's blessings. When we eat with this mindset, we honor both our bodies and our faith.

CHAPTER 7: WELLNESS ROUTINES FOR THE APOSTOLIC WOMAN

Rest, Prayer, and Movement

Taking care of your body and spirit is not just about what you eat. It is also about how you rest, how you connect with God, and how you keep your body moving. These three — rest, prayer, and movement — work together to keep you strong, healthy, and full of life.

Rest

God created our bodies to need rest. Even He rested on the seventh day after creation (Genesis 2:2). Rest is not laziness — it is obedience to God's design. When you sleep well, your body repairs itself, your mind becomes clear, and your mood improves. Try to get enough hours of good sleep each night. Also, take short breaks during the day when you feel tired. Even sitting quietly for a few minutes can refresh your body and spirit.

Prayer

Prayer is food for the soul. It calms your heart, strengthens your faith, and keeps you connected to God. You do not need to wait for the church service to pray. You can talk to God while cooking, walking, or even before sleeping. Prayer is not just asking for things; it is also thanking Him and listening to His voice. As 1 Thessalonians 5:17 says, "Pray without ceasing." The more you pray, the more peace you will have in your daily life.

Movement

Our bodies were made to move. You don't necessarily have to visit the gym or lift heavy weights. Simple activities like walking, stretching, cleaning the house, or playing with your children can keep your body active. Movement helps your heart stay strong, your muscles flexible, and your mind sharp. Proverbs 31 describes the virtuous woman as being hardworking and active — she "sets about her work vigorously; her arms are strong for her tasks" (Proverbs 31:17).

When you balance rest, prayer, and movement, you take care of both your body and spirit. You will have more energy to serve your family, help others, and live your calling as an Apostolic woman. Remember, your body is the temple of the Holy Spirit (1 Corinthians 6:19), so treat it with love and care. Rest when you need to, pray every day, and keep moving — your health and faith will thank you.

Managing Stress Through Faith

Life can sometimes feel heavy. We may have many responsibilities—family, work, ministry, and daily challenges. Stress is something we cannot always avoid, but as an Apostolic woman, we have a special gift: our faith in God. Faith is not just for Sunday services; it is a daily tool to help us stay calm and strong even when things are tough.

The first step to managing stress through faith is learning to give everything to God. The Bible says, "Cast all your cares upon Him, for He cares for you." This means you do not have to carry your worries alone. Whenever you feel overwhelmed, stop for a moment, close your eyes, and speak to God in prayer. You can say, "Lord, I give You this burden. Help me to trust You." This simple habit can bring peace to your heart instantly.

Another way to handle stress is by filling your mind with God's Word. When we study the Bible, we are reminded of God's promises. Verses about His love, protection, and provision can replace fear and worry with peace. Even if you are busy, you can keep one or two short scriptures in your heart and repeat them throughout the day. For example: "The Lord is my shepherd; I shall not want" (Psalm 23:1) or "Be still, and know that I am God" (Psalm 46:10).

Worship is also a powerful stress reliever. Singing praises shifts our focus from problems to God's greatness. You do not need a big choir—just you and your voice is enough. Sing while cooking, cleaning, or walking. Worship reminds your spirit that God is in control.

Finally, surround yourself with faith-filled people. Talking with someone who shares your belief can lift your mood and give you fresh hope. Sometimes, just knowing that someone is praying for you makes the load feel lighter.

Stress may come, but it does not have to control you. With faith, prayer, scripture, and worship, you can walk through hard times with peace in your heart and a smile on your face, knowing God is carrying you every step of the way.

Herbal Remedies and Natural Supplements

God has blessed us with many plants and natural foods that can help our bodies stay strong and healthy. These are not to replace prayer or medical care, but they can be a gentle way to support our health. Herbal remedies and natural supplements have been used for centuries, and many still work well today when used wisely.

When we take care of our bodies, we can serve God and our families better. But it is important to remember—always pray for wisdom before trying anything new, and if you have health problems or take medicine, talk to your doctor first.

Herbs are plants with natural healing properties. Some can help with digestion, others can boost energy, calm the mind, or support the immune system. Natural supplements, like vitamins or minerals, can fill in the gaps when our diet does not provide enough nutrients.

Here is a simple table of common herbs and what they are often used for:

Herb	Common Use
Ginger	Helps with digestion, nausea, and reduces cold symptoms
Garlic	Supports heart health, boosts immunity
Turmeric	Reduces inflammation and supports joint health
Peppermint	Calms upset stomach, eases headaches
Chamomile	Helps relaxation, supports better sleep
Moringa	Boosts energy, rich in vitamins and minerals
Lemongrass	Refreshes the body, supports healthy digestion

You don't need to take many herbs at once. Sometimes, one or two is enough for your body's needs. You can use them as teas, in your cooking, or as capsules from a trusted source.

Also, be mindful of quality. Not all herbs sold in the market are pure. Choose fresh herbs or products from trusted sellers. Pray over them before use, thanking God for the healing He has placed in His creation.

Herbs and supplements work best when combined with a healthy lifestyle—eating balanced meals, drinking enough water, resting well, and staying close to God in prayer. When your body is well, your spirit can serve Him with more strength and joy.

CHAPTER 8: THE POWER OF FASTING

Types of Biblical Fasts

Fasting is not just about skipping food; it is a spiritual discipline that draws us closer to God. In the Bible, fasting was a way to humble oneself before the Lord, seek His direction, or pray for His mercy. Different types of fasts are shown in Scripture, and each one has a purpose.

Here are some common types of Biblical fasts:

1. Complete Fast (No Food, Only Water)

This is when you avoid all food and take only water for a period of time. In Esther 4:16, Queen Esther and the Jews fasted like this when their lives were in danger. This type of fast is intense and should be done only as God leads you and if your health allows.

2. Partial Fast (Certain Foods or Meals)

Sometimes, you may choose to eat only certain foods or avoid specific meals. The "Daniel Fast" in Daniel 10:3 is an example—he ate no meat, sweets, or rich foods for three weeks. This is a good option if you cannot do a complete fast but still want to deny yourself and focus on God.

3. Dry Fast (No Food and No Water)

This is the most extreme type and is usually short, like the one Esther did for three days. It should only be done for a very short period, and only when the Holy Spirit clearly leads you.

4. One-Meal-a-Day Fast

In this fast, you eat only one meal in a day and spend the rest of the time praying and reading God's Word. It's easier on the body but still powerful in the spirit.

5. Corporate or Group Fast

This is when a church, ministry, or group of believers fast together for a common purpose—maybe for revival, healing, or guidance. Joel 2:15-16 talks about calling the whole assembly to fast.

6. Lifestyle or Regular Fasting

Some believers make fasting a normal part of their lives—like skipping a meal every week to pray. This keeps their spirit sharp and their heart humble before God.

Fasting is not about showing off holiness or punishing the body—it is about humbling ourselves to hear from God more clearly. When you fast, always combine it with prayer, worship, and reading the Bible. That is when it becomes powerful.

Fasting for Physical and Spiritual Breakthroughs

Fasting is not just about skipping meals. It is a special time when you tell your body and mind to focus on God instead of food. Many people fast because they are asking God for help, direction, healing, or a big change in their life. The Bible shows us that fasting can open doors for both physical and spiritual breakthroughs.

When you fast, you give your body a break from constant eating. This can help your body rest, repair, and even remove harmful toxins. People often feel lighter, more alert, and more energetic after fasting. Some also experience better health over time because fasting can help the body heal naturally.

But the biggest power of fasting is not physical—it is spiritual. Fasting is like turning up the volume on your prayers. You are telling God, "This is so important to me that I am willing to give up food for a time to seek You." This act of sacrifice moves you into a deeper place of focus and faith.

In the Bible, we see people fasting before making big decisions, during times of danger, or when they needed God's mercy. For example, Queen Esther fasted and prayed before going to the king to save her people. Her courage and fasting brought victory. Similarly, the prophet Daniel fasted for understanding and received clear answers from God.

When you fast for a breakthrough, it's important to also pray and read the Word of God. Without prayer, fasting is just dieting. The real power comes when you connect with God during your fast. Speak to Him about what you need, confess your struggles, and listen for His guidance.

Breakthroughs may come in different ways—some people receive healing, others find peace in a storm, and some get direction for their next step. Sometimes the answer comes quickly, other times God uses the fasting period to prepare your heart for what's ahead.

Fasting is not about forcing God to act. It is about humbling yourself, showing your faith, and aligning your heart with His will. When you do this sincerely, both your body and your spirit can be renewed, and you may experience the breakthrough you have been praying for.

How to Start and Maintain a Fasting Lifestyle

Starting a fasting lifestyle is not as hard as many people think. The main thing is to start small and grow into it. If you try to do a long fast on your first attempt, you may struggle and give up quickly. But if you take it step by step, your body and mind will adjust, and it will become a normal part of your life.

The first step is to choose the type of fast that works for you. You can start with something simple like skipping breakfast and eating only lunch and dinner. This is called intermittent fasting and is one of the easiest ways to begin. Later, you can try longer fasts, like fasting for 24 hours once or twice a week.

The second step is to prepare your body. If you normally eat a lot of sugar and processed foods, start cutting them down before you begin fasting. Eat more fruits, vegetables, whole grains, and natural foods. This will make fasting easier and reduce headaches or tiredness in the first few days.

The third step is to drink enough water. Many people think fasting means no water, but most fasting types allow water, and it's very important. Water helps you stay full, removes toxins from your body, and keeps you from feeling weak. You can also take herbal teas without sugar.

The fourth step is to listen to your body. Fasting should not make you sick. If you feel dizzy, too weak, or have severe pain, it's okay to break your fast and try again later. Your health comes first.

To maintain a fasting lifestyle, make it part of your routine. For example, you can decide that every Monday you will fast until evening. Or you can choose certain hours every day when you don't eat. Over time, your body will get used to it, and it will no longer feel like a struggle.

Finally, stay connected to your purpose. Whether you are fasting for health, spiritual growth, or both, always remind yourself why you are doing it. This will keep you strong, especially when you feel tempted to give up.

Fasting is a journey, not a one-time event. If you start small, stay consistent, and keep your mind focused, it can become a natural and powerful part of your life.

PART 3: APOSTOLIC RECIPES & MEAL PLANS

CHAPTER 9: 7-DAY APOSTOLIC MEAL PLAN

Clean, Simple, and Nourishing Meals

Eating clean and nourishing meals is not about buying expensive foods or cooking complicated recipes. It is about choosing simple, fresh ingredients that will bless your body and keep your mind clear. In the Apostolic lifestyle, food is not just for filling the stomach—it is for strength, health, and honoring God with our bodies.

When we say "clean," we mean food that is as close to the way God made it as possible. This means fresh vegetables, fruits, whole grains, fish, lean meats, nuts, seeds, and herbs. It means reducing packaged snacks, processed sugar, and fried junk. Simple meals are easier for your body to digest, give you steady energy, and help you stay spiritually alert.

"Nourishing" means the food is full of the good things your body needs—vitamins, minerals, healthy fats, and natural fiber. You do not need to eat too much at once. Even a small plate of healthy food can give you strength for the day if it is balanced and made with care.

Here are some tips to keep your meals clean and nourishing:

- Choose fresh over packaged — Whenever possible, buy vegetables, fruits, and grains in their natural state.
- Cook simply — Steaming, boiling, or baking keeps more nutrients in the food than frying.
- Add natural flavors — Use herbs, spices, and a little natural oil (like olive or coconut oil) instead of heavy sauces.
- Eat in moderation — Stop when you are satisfied, not when you are stuffed.
- Stay hydrated — Water is part of a nourishing meal plan. Drink before, during, and after meals.

Eating this way also makes it easier to combine fasting and prayer. When your meals are clean, your body feels lighter, your energy is steady, and your mind stays focused.

The 7-Day Apostolic Meal Plan in this chapter will give you simple recipes and meal ideas that are easy to prepare, affordable, and fit into your daily life. You can mix and match them based on what is available in your area. Remember, it is not just about the food—it is about the heart and discipline behind it. Eat with gratitude, and let each meal be a way to care for the body God has given you.

Breakfast, Lunch, Dinner & Snack Ideas

When planning your Apostolic meals, you don't need to stress or overthink it. The goal is to eat clean, simple, and nourishing food that keeps your body healthy and your spirit focused. This 7-day guide gives you ideas for breakfast, lunch, dinner, and snacks that are easy to prepare and satisfying.

Day 1

• Breakfast: Warm oatmeal with chopped bananas and a sprinkle of cinnamon.

• Lunch: Steamed vegetables with baked sweet potatoes.

• Dinner: Brown rice with lentils and sautéed greens.

• Snack: A handful of roasted groundnuts.

Day 2

• Breakfast: Whole grain bread with avocado spread.

• Lunch: Quinoa salad with cucumbers, tomatoes, and olive oil.

• Dinner: Vegetable soup with carrots, cabbage, and herbs.

• Snack: Fresh mango slices.

Day 3

• Breakfast: Pap (akamu) with almond milk and dates.

• Lunch: Boiled yam with vegetable stew.

- Dinner: Millet porridge with steamed spinach.
- Snack: A small bowl of watermelon.

Day 4

- Breakfast: Rice cakes with peanut butter.
- Lunch: Lentil stew with a side of steamed plantain.
- Dinner: Brown rice with okra soup (light oil, no meat).
- Snack: Apple slices with a few cashew nuts.

Day 5

- Breakfast: Smoothie with banana, spinach, and oats.
- Lunch: Sweet potato mash with vegetable sauce.
- Dinner: Quinoa with stir-fried mixed veggies.
- Snack: A handful of raisins.

Day 6

- Breakfast: Cornmeal porridge with chopped dates.
- Lunch: Vegetable wrap with hummus.
- Dinner: Boiled beans with steamed pumpkin leaves.
- Snack: Fresh pineapple chunks.

Day 7

- Breakfast: Whole grain pancakes with honey drizzle.
- Lunch: Rice and peas with a side of coleslaw.
- Dinner: Sweet corn soup with vegetables.

- Snack: Roasted plantain slices.

These ideas are flexible—you can swap meals around, adjust to your taste, or use what is in season. The key is to keep the meals simple, fresh, and made from natural foods. Eat until you are satisfied, but avoid overeating. Drink plenty of clean water throughout the day, and give thanks before and after each meal.

Scripture for Each Day

When we eat with God's Word in our hearts, our meals become more than food — they become moments of worship. Reading a scripture before or after eating reminds us that our strength, health, and daily bread all come from the Lord. Here is a simple plan for 7 days. You can read these verses out loud during your meal times, or just meditate on them in your heart.

Day 1 – Philippians 4:13

"I can do all things through Christ who strengthens me."
Say this before you start your day. It will remind you that with God, you have the strength to make healthy choices and live in peace.

Day 2 – Psalm 107:9

"For He satisfies the thirsty & fills the hungry with good things."
A perfect verse for breakfast or lunch. It will help you remember that God wants to nourish you, body and soul.

Day 3 – Matthew 6:11

"Give us this day our daily bread."
A short but powerful prayer. You can say this at dinner to thank God for His daily provision.

Day 4 – 1 Corinthians 10:31

"So whether you drink or eat or whatever you do, ensure you do it for the glory of God."

Read this before eating to keep your heart focused on gratitude and godly living.

Day 5 – Isaiah 55:2

"Listen, listen to me, and eat what is good, and you will delight in the richest of fare."

This verse reminds us to choose what is wholesome — both in food and in life.

Day 6 – Psalm 34:8

"Taste and see that the Lord is good; blessed is the one who takes refuge in Him."

Say this as you eat, and let your meal be a reminder of God's goodness in every part of life.

Day 7 – John 6:35

"Jesus declared, 'I am the bread of life. Whoever comes to me will never go hungry, & whoever believes in me will never be thirsty.'"

A perfect verse for a Sunday meal, reminding you that Jesus is the true source of satisfaction.

You can rotate these verses every week or choose new ones from your Bible. The key is to keep God in the center of your meals and daily life.

CHAPTER 10: FAITH-BASED RECIPES FOR WOMEN

Breakfasts: Faith-Filled Mornings

A good morning starts with two things — talking to God and having a healthy meal. Breakfast is not just about filling the stomach. It's also a way to thank God for giving you another day. When you wake up, your body needs energy, and your spirit needs encouragement. That is why starting your day with both prayer and a nourishing meal is important.

Think of breakfast as your morning offering — you give your body what it needs so you can serve God and others well during the day. Even if you are busy, you can still prepare something quick, healthy, and tasty. You don't need to spend hours in the kitchen. With the right ingredients, you can make meals that keep you strong and full of life.

Here are some simple breakfast ideas you can try. You can even say a short prayer as you cook, asking God to bless your food and your day.

1. Banana Oat Pancakes

Ingredients:

- 1 ripe banana
- 1 egg
- 3 tbsp oats
- 1 tsp honey (optional)

Instructions:

1. Mash banana in a bowl.
2. Add egg and oats, mix well.
3. Pour small amounts into a pan and cook for 1–2 minutes each side.
4. Serve warm.

2. Boiled Eggs & Avocado Toast

Ingredients:

- 2 boiled eggs
- 1 slice whole-grain bread
- ½ avocado, mashed
- Pinch of salt

Instructions:

1. Spread avocado on toast.
2. Slice boiled eggs on top.
3. Add salt to taste.

3. Fruit & Yogurt Parfait

Ingredients:

- ½ cup plain yogurt
- ½ cup chopped fruits (banana, apple, berries)
- 1 tbsp granola

Instructions:

1. Put yogurt in a glass.
2. Add fruits and granola on top.
3. Eat fresh.

Every bite you take in the morning should remind you of God's blessings. A simple breakfast, enjoyed with a thankful heart, can give you the strength and joy you need to shine all day.

Lunches: Light & Holy Midday Meals

Lunch is the time when our bodies and minds need a gentle refuel. It's the middle of the day, and for many women, this is also the time when life feels the busiest. But even in the rush, we can pause, breathe, and invite God's peace into our meal.

A light and holy midday meal is not just about the food—it's about slowing down enough to thank God for His blessings. It's about eating in a way that gives energy but doesn't make you feel heavy or tired afterward. When we choose fresh, wholesome ingredients, we honor the body God gave us.

Faith-based lunches can be simple but still nourishing. They can be a time for prayer or reflection, even if it's just a quick "Thank You, Lord" before eating. Some women like to read a short Bible verse before lunch or listen to uplifting music while they prepare their meal. This helps turn lunchtime into a little sacred moment in the day.

When planning your midday meal, think of balance—some protein to keep you full, fresh vegetables for health, and a little healthy fat for energy. It doesn't have to be fancy; even simple foods, when prepared with love and gratitude, become a blessing.

Here are two easy recipes to inspire your faith-filled lunch:

1. Grilled Chicken & Veggie Wrap

1 small whole wheat tortilla

½ cup grilled chicken breast (sliced)

½ cup mixed salad greens

2 tbsp hummus or light cream cheese

Salt and pepper to taste

Instructions:

Spread hummus on the tortilla, layer with chicken and greens, season lightly, roll up, and enjoy. Say a brief prayer of thanks before eating.

2. Lentil & Spinach Soup

½ cup dried lentils, rinsed

2 cups vegetable broth

1 cup fresh spinach

½ chopped onion

Salt, pepper, and a pinch of turmeric

Instructions:

Boil lentils with broth and onion until tender. Add spinach and season to taste. Let it simmer for 5 minutes. Serve warm while reflecting on God's goodness.

Even in the busiest afternoons, choosing light, wholesome foods keeps the body strong and the heart thankful. And remember—every meal is an opportunity to nourish not just your body, but your soul too.

Dinners: Comforting & Blessed Evening Meals

Dinner is not just about filling your stomach at the end of the day.

It's a quiet moment to rest, reflect, and thank God for His blessings.

A peaceful dinner can be a reminder that God's care follows you from sunrise to sunset.

Faith-based dinners don't have to be complicated or fancy.

Think of meals that are light enough to help you sleep well, but still nutritious enough to nourish your body.

It's about ending the day feeling satisfied — both in body and spirit.

Here are a few simple tips for making your evening meal feel blessed:

• Pray before eating – A short, heartfelt prayer thanking God for the day and the food in front of you can bring peace to your heart.

• Keep it light – Avoid heavy, greasy foods at night so your body rests instead of working hard to digest.

• Add a touch of nature – Fresh herbs, vegetables, and simple proteins give your body God-made nutrients.

• Eat slowly – Enjoy every bite without rushing. It's not just food — it's God's provision.

Sample Blessed Dinner Ideas

1. Baked Salmon with Steamed Spinach

Season salmon with olive oil, lemon, and herbs. Bake until tender and serve with fresh spinach. Rich in Omega-3 for heart health.

2. Chicken & Vegetable Soup

Slow-cooked chicken with carrots, celery, onions, and a little ginger. Comforting and gentle on the stomach.

3. Lentil & Tomato Stew (Great for vegetarians)

Lentils simmered with tomatoes, garlic, and fresh herbs. High in fiber and protein, but still light for nighttime.

4. Grilled Veggie Plate with Brown Rice

Zucchini, bell peppers, and mushrooms drizzled with olive oil and grilled. Serve with a small side of brown rice.

When you make dinner, remember that it's not just the recipe that matters — it's the love and gratitude you put into it.

Even if it's a simple bowl of soup, when cooked with a thankful heart, it becomes a true blessing for the body and soul.

End your day with food that leaves you feeling calm, loved, and cared for — because you are.

Snacks: Little Bites with Big Blessings

Sometimes, all we need in the middle of the day is a little something to keep us going — not too heavy, but enough to give us energy and a smile. Snacks can be more than just food; they can be a little reminder of God's goodness in the small things. These "little bites with big blessings" are perfect for tea breaks, prayer moments, or even as a light pick-me-up while you read your Bible or chat with a friend.

The key here is to keep it simple, healthy, and uplifting. You don't need to spend hours in the kitchen to make snacks that bless your body and spirit. Many of these recipes are quick to prepare, with ingredients that you may already have at home.

Here are some ideas you can enjoy:

1. Fruit & Nut Blessing Cups

•   A small bowl of chopped apples, banana slices, and a handful of unsalted nuts.

•   Drizzle with a little honey for sweetness.

•   As you eat, thank God for each fruit and nut, remembering how He provides variety in life.

2. Holy Hummus Dip

•   Blend chickpeas, olive oil, garlic, and a squeeze of lemon juice.

• Serve with carrot sticks, cucumber slices, or whole grain crackers.

• Perfect for a quiet moment of reflection while feeding your body something wholesome.

3. Date & Almond Energy Balls

• Blend dates, almonds, and a pinch of cinnamon.

• Roll into small bite-sized balls.

• These little treats are naturally sweet and full of energy — perfect before a prayer meeting or Bible study.

4. Faithful Yogurt Parfait

• Layer plain yogurt with fresh berries and a sprinkle of granola.

• A light but filling snack that can also double as a quick breakfast.

• As you layer the ingredients, reflect on how God layers blessings in our lives.

Encouragement for Snack Time:

Snacks can be more than just something to fill your stomach. They can be a pause in your day to slow down, breathe, and give thanks. Even a handful of nuts or a few slices of fruit can turn into a holy moment when you pair it with gratitude.

Remember, our bodies are temples of the Holy Spirit — so every little bite is a chance to honor Him with what we eat.

Dinners: Nourishing Evening Meals to End the Day with Peace

Dinner is often the time when families gather, talk about their day, and share laughter. For women who want to keep their meals both healthy and faith-filled, the evening table can be a place of blessing and renewal. After a long day, the goal is to serve meals that are light on the stomach, gentle on the body, but full of flavor and goodness.

Faith-based dinners are not just about food—they are about creating a peaceful atmosphere where gratitude is the main seasoning. When you eat in thankfulness, you enjoy your food more, and your heart feels lighter. Keep your plates colorful with vegetables, lean proteins, and whole grains. Add herbs and spices that bring healing, like garlic for the heart, ginger for digestion, or basil for calmness.

You can prepare dishes that remind you of God's creation— fresh fish from the waters, leafy greens from the earth, and grains from the fields. For example, a simple grilled fish with steamed vegetables can be as satisfying as any heavy meal. If you enjoy plant-based options, lentil stew with carrots and spinach makes a hearty choice without feeling too heavy before bedtime.

Here are four simple, faith-filled dinner recipes you can use right away. Each one is quick, plain, and made with easy ingredients. Say a short prayer before you eat, then enjoy.

1) Coconut Tilapia with Garden Veggies

Serves: 2 • Time: 20–25 min

Ingredients: 2 tilapia fillets, 1 cup coconut milk, 1 small onion (sliced), 1 tomato (chopped), handful spinach, 1 clove garlic (crushed), pinch salt.

Instructions: Heat a little oil in pan. Fry onion and garlic until soft. Add tomato, coconut milk and salt. Put tilapia in the sauce, cover and simmer 8–10 minutes. Stir in spinach for 1 minute. Serve warm.

Short prayer: "Lord, bless this meal and make it strength for Your work."

2) One-Pot Brown Rice with Greens and Smoked Fish

Serves: 3 • Time: 30–35 min

Ingredients: 1 cup brown rice, 2 cups water, 1 cup chopped pumpkin leaves (ugu) or spinach, 1 small smoked fish (flaked), 1 onion, salt.

Instructions: Sauté onion in pot, add rice and water, bring to boil then simmer 25 min. When rice is nearly done, stir in greens and smoked fish, cover 3–4 minutes. Fluff and serve.
Short prayer: "Thank You, Lord, for daily bread."

3) Baked Sweet Potato & Egg Bowl
Serves: 2 • Time: 35–40 min (mostly baking)
Ingredients: 2 medium sweet potatoes, 2 eggs, handful steamed greens, pinch pepper and salt.

Instructions: Bake sweet potatoes 30–35 min at 200°C (or until soft). Boil or fry eggs as you like. Split potatoes, top with greens and egg. Season lightly.
Short prayer: "Lord, renew my strength as I eat."

4) Warm Veggie & Black-Eyed Pea Stir
Serves: 2 • Time: 20 min
Ingredients: 1 cup cooked black-eyed peas, 1 bell pepper (sliced), 1 carrot (sliced), handful kale, 1 tbsp olive oil, salt.

Instructions: Heat oil, stir-fry carrot and pepper 5 min. Add kale and beans, sauté 3–4 min until warm. Season and serve.
Short prayer: "Thank You, Lord, for this healthy food."

Herbal Teas & Healing Drinks

Sometimes, healing and comfort can be found in something as simple as a warm cup of tea. For many women, especially those who believe in faith and natural living, herbal teas are more than just drinks — they are a way to care for the body, calm the mind, and feed the spirit.

Herbal teas and healing drinks are made from leaves, flowers, roots, seeds, or even dried fruits. They are caffeine-free (most of the time) and full of natural goodness. Drinking them regularly can help with digestion, sleep, stress, immunity, and even hormone balance.

One beautiful thing about these teas is that they can be enjoyed during quiet prayer or meditation times. Holding a warm cup in your hands, breathing in the aroma, and slowly sipping can become a small daily ritual that brings both physical relief and spiritual peace.

Here are some examples of simple herbal teas and healing drinks you can make at home:

Ginger Tea – Fresh ginger slices boiled in water, great for digestion, nausea, and warming the body.

Peppermint Tea – Calms the stomach, eases bloating, and refreshes the mind.

Chamomile Tea – Helps with relaxation and better sleep.

Lemon & Honey Water – Boosts immunity, refreshes, and soothes sore throats.

Turmeric Milk (Golden Milk) – Warm milk with turmeric and a pinch of black pepper, good for inflammation and joint pain.

How to Make Basic Herbal Tea

- Boil 1–2 cups of water.
- Add 1–2 tsps of dried herbs (or a small handful of fresh herbs).
- Cover and let it steep for 5–10 minutes (longer for stronger flavor).
- Strain, add honey if you like, and sip slowly.

When making these teas, remember to speak life over your body. Thank God for the healing power in nature and trust that every sip is helping you in some way. Faith is like tea — the longer it sits in your heart, the stronger it becomes.

You can drink these in the morning to start your day with energy, in the afternoon to refresh, or at night to relax before bed. Keep it simple, natural, and consistent, and you will soon notice how something so small can make a big difference.

CHAPTER 11: RECIPES FOR FASTING DAYS

Light Soups, Broths & Juice Ideas

On fasting days, your body is resting from heavy digestion, so you need meals that are light, gentle, and full of hydration. Light soups, broths, and fresh juices are perfect because they keep you satisfied without overworking your stomach. They also give you vitamins, minerals, and fluids to keep your energy up.

When I'm fasting, I like to think of these meals as "soft fuel" for my body. They go in easily, they feel light, and they still give me the goodness I need to keep going through the day. The secret is to keep them fresh, simple, and not overloaded with salt, sugar, or oil.

Here are some ideas you can try:

1. Clear Vegetable Broth
Boil carrots, celery, onion, garlic, and a pinch of herbs in water until the flavors come out. Strain the vegetables and sip the warm broth. It's comforting and hydrating.

2. Light Chicken Broth

If you're not strictly plant-based, simmer chicken bones with onion, ginger, and a little parsley. Strain and drink the clear broth. It gives gentle protein and warmth.

3. Spinach & Garlic Light Soup

Boil a handful of spinach with chopped garlic in water for 3–4 minutes. Add a pinch of salt and drink while warm. Very quick and soothing.

4. Lemon & Mint Water

For hot weather fasting, squeeze fresh lemon into cool water and add a few mint leaves. It refreshes you and supports digestion.

5. Simple Green Juice

Blend cucumber, celery, spinach, and apple with cold water. Strain if you want it lighter. This is like a green vitamin drink.

6. Ginger-Carrot Juice

Blend fresh carrots with a small piece of ginger and water. Strain and serve chilled. It's sweet, a little spicy, and energizing.

Tips for Fasting Day Recipes:

- Keep flavors mild; your stomach is resting.
- Avoid heavy oil, dairy, and too much seasoning.
- Drink slowly and listen to your body.
- Keep portions small; you can always make more if you're still hungry.

Fasting days don't have to feel like punishment. With light soups, clean broths, and fresh juices, you can still enjoy warm comfort or cool refreshment while giving your body a gentle break.

Fasting-Friendly Foods

When you are fasting, you are not eating for many hours. This means that when it is time to eat, you need foods that are gentle on your stomach, give you good energy, and keep you full for a while. The goal is to choose simple, healthy foods that do not make you feel heavy or tired.

One of the best fasting-friendly foods is soups. Warm vegetable soup, chicken broth, or a light fish soup is easy to digest and helps your body rehydrate after fasting. Soups also give you important minerals and vitamins without overloading your stomach.

Smoothies are another good choice. You can blend fruits like banana, berries, or mango with plain yogurt or milk. Adding a spoon of peanut butter or chia seeds can make it more filling. Smoothies are soft, quick to make, and perfect when you don't feel like chewing a lot after fasting.

Eggs are also a great option. Boiled, scrambled, or made into a simple omelet with spinach or tomatoes, they are full of protein and keep you satisfied without feeling too heavy.

If you want something fresh, salads are a smart pick. You can make a simple salad with cucumbers, lettuce, tomatoes, and a light dressing. Add a boiled egg or some grilled chicken for extra strength.

For snacks, go for nuts and seeds like almonds, walnuts, sunflower seeds, or pumpkin seeds. These give you healthy fats that keep your energy steady. But remember, eat them in small amounts because they are high in calories.

Whole grains like oatmeal, quinoa, or brown rice are also gentle and filling. You can make a small bowl with some vegetables or a little meat for your first meal after fasting.

Fruits such as watermelon, papaya, and oranges are hydrating and sweet naturally. They give you quick energy without processed sugar.

And finally, do not forget water. After fasting, drink water slowly before eating to help your stomach adjust. You can also take herbal tea or coconut water for extra hydration.

The key is to keep your first meal light and balanced, then slowly move to heavier meals if you are still hungry. Fasting days are not about stuffing your stomach when you finally eat—they are about choosing foods that make your body feel good, fresh, and nourished.

Prayer & Fasting Journal Prompts

One thing that makes fasting more powerful is writing down your thoughts, prayers, and feelings as you go through it. A journal is not just a book — it's your private space where you can pour out your heart to God, write your struggles, and celebrate your wins. It also helps you stay focused when you feel tired, hungry, or distracted.

Here are some simple prompts you can use during your fasting days. You can write every morning, during breaks, or before bed. There is no right or wrong way — just be honest and write from your heart.

Morning Prompts (to start your fasting day)

- "God, this is what I'm believing You for today…"
- "Lord, I give You my worries about…"
- "I am thankful today for…"
- "The scripture that speaks to me today is…"
- "My intention for today's fast is…"

Midday Prompts (when you need strength)

- "Right now, I'm feeling…"
- "Lord, help me stay focused on…"
- "I want to hear Your voice about…"
- "One thing I'm learning about myself is…"

- "This verse gives me peace right now…"

Evening Prompts (to close your fasting day)
- "Lord, thank You for helping me through today…"
- "The moment that was hardest for me today was…"
- "I felt Your presence when…"
- "One thing I will remember from today is…"
- "My prayer for tomorrow is…"

Extra Reflection Prompts (you can use anytime)
- "What is God teaching me in this season?"
- "What habits is God helping me to break?"
- "What new blessings have I noticed this week?"
- "How has my faith grown since I started fasting?"
- "What is one fear I'm giving to God completely?"

You don't have to write full pages — even a few sentences are enough. The goal is to keep your mind and heart connected to God while you fast. Over time, when you read back your journal, you'll see how much you've grown, the prayers God has answered, and the strength He has given you.

PART 4: SPIRITUAL GROWTH & ENCOURAGEMENT

CHAPTER 12: SPIRITUAL GROWTH THROUGH DIET

Eating with Gratitude

Food is not just about filling our stomachs — it is also about feeding our soul. The way we eat can affect how we feel inside, not only physically but also spiritually. Eating with gratitude means being truly thankful for the food on your plate, the hands that prepared it, and the source it came from.

In today's fast life, many people eat in a hurry — in the car, while scrolling on their phones, or even while standing. When this happens, we often forget to appreciate the meal itself. But when you pause, breathe, and take a moment to give thanks, you connect to something bigger than yourself. It can be a quiet "thank you" in your heart, a short prayer, or simply a deep breath before you start eating.

Gratitude changes the way you see food. A simple plate of vegetables becomes more than just vegetables — it becomes a blessing. You start to think about the farmer who grew them, the rain that watered them, the sun that made them grow, and the effort it took to bring them to your table. This awareness can bring peace and joy, even before the first bite.

Eating with gratitude also helps you slow down. You chew more carefully, enjoy the taste, and notice the smell and texture of your food. This not only helps your digestion but also makes you feel satisfied with less. Over time, you may find yourself craving healthier foods naturally because you respect what you put into your body.

For spiritual growth, it's not just what you eat, but how you eat. A calm and thankful mind while eating can help you feel more balanced, patient, and connected to your inner self. It turns every meal into a small act of meditation and respect — for the earth, for the people around you, and for your own body.

You can start small. Before your next meal, close your eyes for a few seconds. Think of at least one thing you are thankful for about that food. This little habit, repeated every day, can help you grow spiritually while also improving your relationship with food.

When you eat with gratitude, every meal becomes a reminder that life itself is a gift — and that is true nourishment.

Renewing Your Mind Daily

Renewing your mind daily is like giving your thoughts a fresh bath every morning. Just as your body needs food to stay strong, your mind needs the right "food" to stay positive, peaceful, and focused on the right things. What you think about all day shapes your mood, your actions, and even your health.

A clean and healthy diet is not just for the body—it helps the mind too. When you eat fresh, wholesome foods, your brain works better. You can think clearly, make better decisions, and feel more in control. For example, too much sugar and processed food can make you feel tired, moody, and even anxious. But fresh fruits, vegetables, lean meats, and natural herbs can give you calm energy and help you think straight.

Renewing your mind is not only about food, but also about what you feed your heart and thoughts. Every day, you can choose to start with uplifting words—maybe a short prayer, a Bible verse, or a positive affirmation like, "Today I choose peace and joy." This sets the tone for the whole day.

It also helps to protect your mind from negative "junk food." Just as you avoid spoiled food to protect your body, avoid harmful thoughts, bad news, and constant complaining. If you let these in every day, they will weaken your mind just like unhealthy food weakens the body.

Here's a simple daily practice:

• Morning: Eat a clean breakfast, drink water, and think of three things you are grateful for.

• Afternoon: Take a short pause, breathe deeply, and remind yourself of something positive.

• Evening: Before bed, reflect on your day and let go of any anger or stress.

When your mind is renewed daily, it becomes easier to make good choices—not just with food, but in every part of life. You'll notice more peace, more joy, and more self-control. A healthy diet feeds your body, but a renewed mind feeds your soul. Both work together to help you grow spiritually and live with purpose.

Growing in Faith through Discipline

Faith is not just about what we believe—it is also about how we live. Discipline is one of the most important tools that helps our faith grow strong. Without discipline, it is easy to give up when life gets hard. But with discipline, we stay focused on God and His plan for us, even when we face challenges.

When it comes to our diet, discipline means making the right choices every day, even when we feel tempted to do otherwise. It is not always easy to say "no" to unhealthy food or "yes" to the meals that truly nourish our bodies. But every time we choose what is good for us, we are training ourselves to be stronger—not just in body, but in spirit. This same self-control also helps us in other areas of life, like prayer, studying God's Word, and resisting bad habits.

Growing in faith through discipline is like planting seeds in a garden. At first, it may seem like nothing is happening. You make good food choices, you pray more often, you keep your thoughts on positive things. But over time, the small daily actions begin to grow into something beautiful. Your health improves. Your mind becomes clearer. Your heart becomes more peaceful. And most importantly, your trust in God becomes deeper.

Discipline also teaches us to depend on God. There will be days when our strength feels weak, and we want to return to old habits. But those are the moments we can pray, "Lord, help me." Each time we lean on Him, our faith is built stronger.

Remember, discipline is not about punishing yourself. It is about loving yourself enough to care for your body and soul the way God wants you to. Every healthy choice you make is an act of faith—a way of saying, "Lord, I believe You have the best plan for my life."

With time, discipline becomes part of who you are. You no longer see it as a burden, but as a blessing. And as you grow in discipline, you will notice your faith growing too—strong, steady, and unshakable.

CHAPTER 13: ENCOURAGEMENT FOR THE APOSTOLIC WOMAN

Scriptures for Strength

There are times when life feels heavy. You may feel tired, discouraged, or even alone in your walk with God. In those moments, the best place to run to is the Word of God. The Bible is like food for your spirit. It gives you strength when your own strength is gone.

Here are some powerful scriptures you can hold on to when you need encouragement:

Isaiah 40:31 – "But they that wait upon the Lord shall renew their strength; they shall mount up with wings as eagles; they shall run, and not be weary; and they shall walk, and not faint." This verse reminds you that waiting on God is never wasted time. He will nourish you with new strength to keep going.

Philippians 4:13 – "I can do all things through Christ which strengtheneth me."
No matter how hard something looks, with Christ in you, you can make it through.

Psalm 46:1 – "God is our refuge and strength, a very present help in trouble."

God is not far away. He is close, ready to help you right now.

2 Timothy 1:7 – "For God hath not given us the spirit of fear; but of power, & of love, & of a sound mind."

Fear is not from God. He has given you courage, love, & peace of mind.

Joshua 1:9 – "Be strong & of a good courage; be not afraid, neither be thou dismayed: for the Lord thy God is with thee whithersoever thou goest."

God is with you everywhere you go, so there is no need to fear.

When you read these scriptures, don't just read them with your eyes—speak them out loud. Let the words enter your heart. Say them when you wake up in the morning. Say them when you feel weak. Say them before you sleep at night.

The more you speak and believe these words, the more you will see your strength grow. Remember, you are not just a woman—you are a daughter of the Most High God. And He has already given you everything you need to stand strong.

Overcoming Discouragement & Temptation

Every Apostolic woman will face times when she feels tired, weak, or even ready to give up. Ministry, family, and personal life can sometimes feel heavy. You may pray, serve, and give your all, yet still feel like you are not doing enough. This is when discouragement tries to enter your heart.

Discouragement often comes quietly. It can be through a negative comment from someone, a prayer that seems unanswered, or a plan that fails. The enemy uses it to make you doubt yourself, your calling, and even God's promises. But you must remember—discouragement is not from God. He has not given you the spirit of fear or defeat, but of power, love, and a sound mind (2 Timothy 1:7).

When discouragement comes, go back to God's Word. Speak scriptures out loud. Remind yourself that God is faithful. Take a moment to worship, even if you do not feel like it. Worship shifts your focus from the problem to the One who can solve it.

Temptation is another challenge. It may come in many forms—pride, anger, bitterness, gossip, or the desire to compromise your values. The enemy knows where you are weakest and will try to use it against you. That is why you must guard your heart daily through prayer, fasting, and staying close to God's presence.

When you feel tempted, do not try to fight in your own strength. Ask the Holy Spirit to help you. Sometimes the best way to overcome temptation is to avoid the situation completely. Joseph did not stay to explain himself when Potiphar's wife tempted him—he ran (Genesis 39:12).

Also, keep the right people around you. Have friends and mentors who can pray for you, encourage you, and correct you when needed. A strong support system can help you rise quickly when you fall.

Most importantly, remember that both discouragement and temptation are temporary battles. They do not define you. Your strength is not in your own ability but in God's power working inside you. Keep your eyes on Jesus, and you will keep moving forward, no matter how many obstacles try to stop you.

Staying the Course with God

Walking with God is not always a straight, smooth road. Sometimes the path feels narrow, lonely, and full of obstacles. But as an apostolic woman, you are called to keep going, no matter what comes your way. Staying the course with God means holding on to Him through the highs and the lows, trusting His plan even when you do not understand everything.

The enemy will try to distract you. Life will bring challenges that make you feel tired or question your calling. People may not always understand your journey. But remember, you are not walking alone. God is right there with you. Every step you take in faith is noticed by Him.

To stay the course, you must keep your eyes on Jesus. Just like Peter began to sink when he looked at the waves instead of Jesus, we too can lose focus if we let problems consume us. When your mind is filled with worries, go back to prayer. Talk to your God like you talk to a friend. Read His Word daily, even if it's just a few verses, and remind yourself of His promises.

Another way to stay strong is to stay connected with other believers. Do not isolate yourself. Find people who encourage your faith, who will pray for you, and who will remind you of God's truth when you feel weak.

Be patient with yourself. Growth takes time. Sometimes you will feel strong, other times you may feel like you are barely moving forward. But progress is still progress, no matter how small.

Finally, never forget the reason you started this journey — your love for God and His love for you. This love is your anchor. It will hold you steady when life's storms rage.

You are called, chosen, and empowered by God. If you stay faithful, keep trusting Him, and refuse to give up, you will finish your race with joy. The reward at the end will be worth every trial you faced along the way. Keep pressing forward.

CHAPTER 14: CONCLUSION

We have come to the end of this book, but the journey of walking with God never ends. As an apostolic woman, you are called to live a life of purpose, faith, and obedience. This is not just about titles or positions—it is about having a heart that is fully surrendered to God, no matter where you are or what you do.

You may face challenges, feel lonely at times, or even wonder if you are making any difference. But remember, God sees every effort you make for Him. He knows the sacrifices you give, the prayers you whisper, and the tears you shed. None of it is wasted.

Walking with God is not always easy. There will be days when you feel tired or discouraged. But the secret is to keep going—one step at a time, one day at a time. Stay connected to God in prayer, hold on to His Word, and surround yourself with people who will encourage you to stay strong in your faith.

Never forget that your work in the Lord is not in vain. Whether you are preaching to many, praying for one person, or simply living a godly life in front of your family, you are planting seeds for eternity.

This book may end here, but your story is still being written by God's own hand. Continue to trust Him even when the road is unclear. Continue to say "yes" to His call, even when it feels uncomfortable. Continue to love people, even when they do not understand you.

You are not alone in this journey. God is with you, and He will finish the good work He has started in you. So rise each day with courage, keep your eyes on Jesus, and never forget—you were chosen for such a time as this.

Your life is a light. Let it shine.

Printed in Dunstable, United Kingdom